# ZOOM!

## Human Body

First published in 2002 by Orpheus Books Ltd.,
2 Church Green, Witney, Oxfordshire, OX28 4AW

Copyright © 2002 Orpheus Books Ltd.

**Created and produced by** Nicholas Harris and
Claire Aston, Orpheus Books Ltd.

**Text** Nicholas Harris

**Consultant** Steve Parker, Scientific Fellow of the
Zoological Society

**Illustrated by** Inklink, Firenze

**Other illustrators** Giuliano Fornari, Debra Woodward

ISBN 1 901323 41 2

A CIP record for this book is available from the British
Library.

Printed and bound in Malaysia.

# ZOOM!

# Human Body

*orpheus*

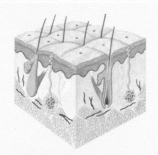

# CONTENTS

# LET'S ZOOM!

When you use the zoom feature on a camera, you bring pictures from distance to close-up without moving it. For example, you can capture the image of a butterfly on a leaf while keeping your distance. This book works in exactly the same way.

Let's imagine you were pointing a camera at a sleeping child. Now zoom in to one part of his body—his wrist. The illustration on pages 8 and 9 shows what you might see in your viewfinder—a mosquito biting the child. Resist your natural instinct to brush it away and carry on zooming! The towering columns that are the child's downy body hairs rear into view. Go beneath the skin, and there are the tiny tubes through which his blood runs. Zoom into the bloodstream and you'll see the cells that make up the blood coursing through those tubes. Keep zooming and you'll discover a cell nucleus, the chromosomes inside that nucleus and eventually the DNA molecule that winds around the chromosomes.

It's a fascinating journey through the human body, yet you will not have to move one millimetre! And you will discover some amazing things about your insides that only this incredible *zooming* book can show you . . .

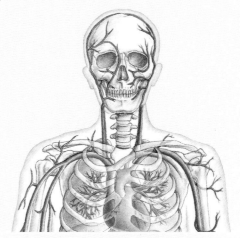

# A SLEEPING CHILD . . .

A young child sleeps. While he does so, all his body's working parts continue to function. His digestive organs, including the stomach, intestines and liver, sort out the nutrients, the substances useful to the body, from the food he has eaten *(see page 22)*. His body has a constant need for oxygen, so he breathes air, his lungs alternately absorbing oxygen and expelling carbon dioxide *(see page 25)*. His heart still beats, pumping blood, which carries nutrients and oxygen to all parts of his body *(see page 24)*.

Even his brain is active, controlling his digestion, breathing and heart beat, and many other things besides *(see page 26)*.

The human body is an amazing natural machine. If you give it food, water, air and warmth, it can walk, talk, think and produce more of its own kind. Flesh and bones, blood and organs are all superbly designed to act together and make it a moving, feeling and clever being!

The human body is made of tiny building blocks called cells. There are more than 100 million million of them. In this book, we will zoom down into the very heart of one of these cells . . .

ZOOM DOWN TO THE SKIN, THE BODY'S OUTER LAYER

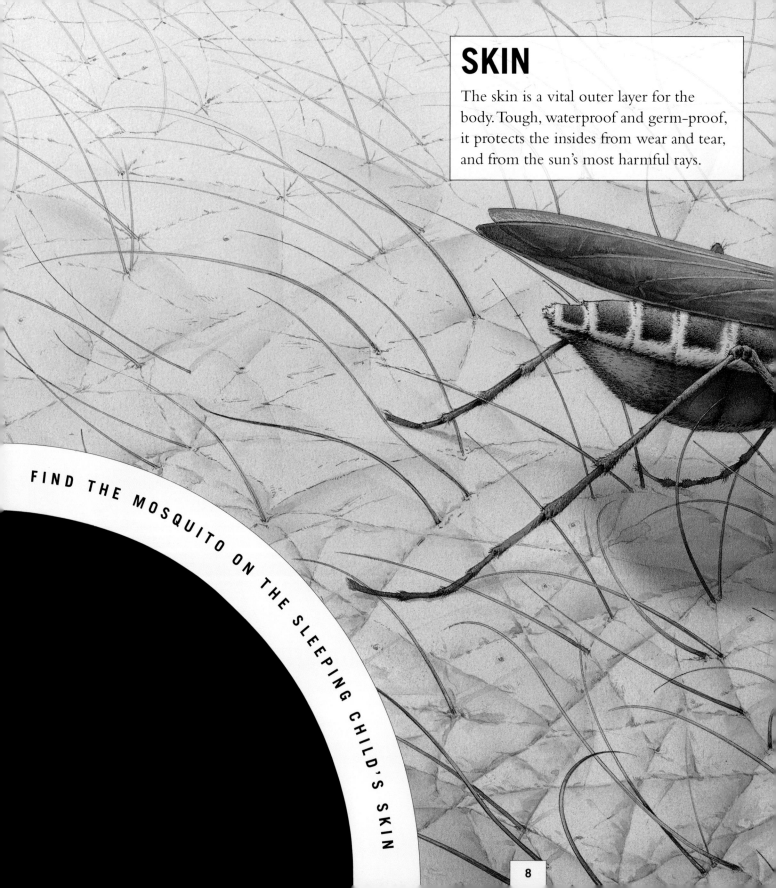

# SKIN

The skin is a vital outer layer for the body. Tough, waterproof and germ-proof, it protects the insides from wear and tear, and from the sun's most harmful rays.

FIND THE MOSQUITO ON THE SLEEPING CHILD'S SKIN

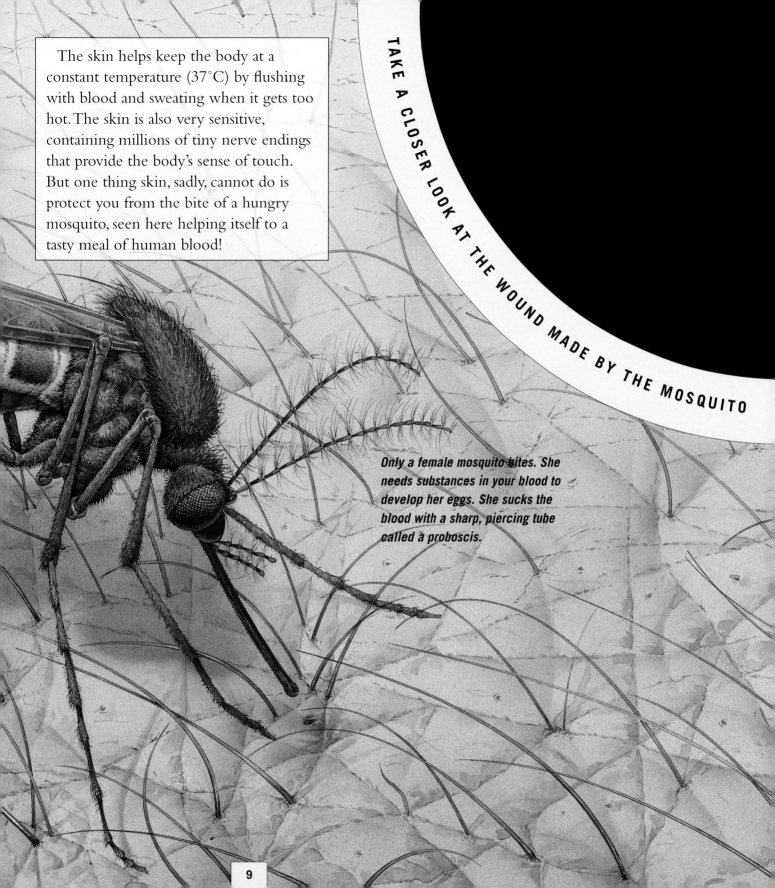

The skin helps keep the body at a constant temperature (37°C) by flushing with blood and sweating when it gets too hot. The skin is also very sensitive, containing millions of tiny nerve endings that provide the body's sense of touch. But one thing skin, sadly, cannot do is protect you from the bite of a hungry mosquito, seen here helping itself to a tasty meal of human blood!

Only a female mosquito bites. She needs substances in your blood to develop her eggs. She sucks the blood with a sharp, piercing tube called a proboscis.

FIND WHERE THE MOSQUITO PIERCED THE SKIN

# HAIR

Skin may feel quite smooth, but when we zoom in close it looks like an amazing, craggy landscape of hills and valleys. There are huge pits, each sprouting a gigantic column of hair (seen here about 750 times their actual size). At this magnification you can see that those shiny, thin strands have, in fact, a rough, scaly surface.

Hair is made from keratin, the same substance that forms fingernails, toenails and the tough outer surface of the skin. The visible part, called the shaft, is actually dead tissue. The live part is at

*The mosquito's bite has made a cut in the skin. The blood clots to form a plug, while white blood cells get to work to destroy any germs.*

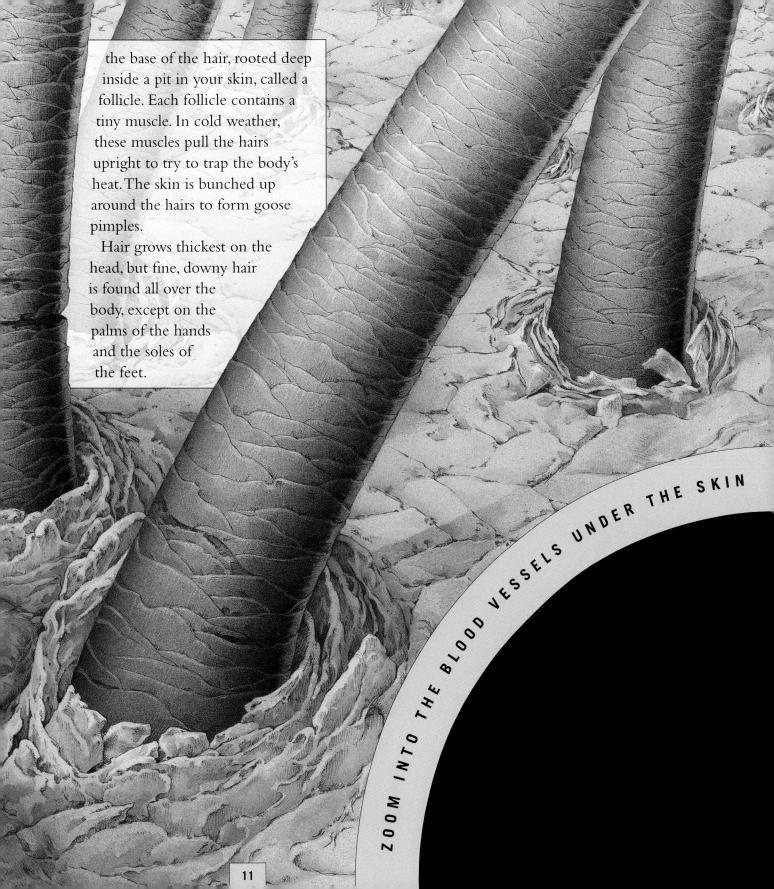

the base of the hair, rooted deep inside a pit in your skin, called a follicle. Each follicle contains a tiny muscle. In cold weather, these muscles pull the hairs upright to try to trap the body's heat. The skin is bunched up around the hairs to form goose pimples.

Hair grows thickest on the head, but fine, downy hair is found all over the body, except on the palms of the hands and the soles of the feet.

ZOOM INTO THE BLOOD VESSELS UNDER THE SKIN

Arteriole

A BLOOD VESSEL HAS BEEN PUNCTURED BY THE BITE

# CAPILLARIES

Blood flows to every part of the body. Pumped by the heart, it circulates through a huge network of tubes called blood vessels *(see page 24)*. Arteries are vessels that carry blood from the heart, while veins carry blood to the heart. Most arteries contain bright red blood that is rich in oxygen. They divide into smaller branches called arterioles, which in turn divide into tiny tubes called capillaries. Oxygen and nutrients can pass from the capillaries into cells, while waste flows in the opposite direction. Capillaries link up to venules. These carry blood of a bluish colour that is low in oxygen.

ZOOM IN TO DISCOVER WHAT BLOOD IS MADE OF

*Venule*

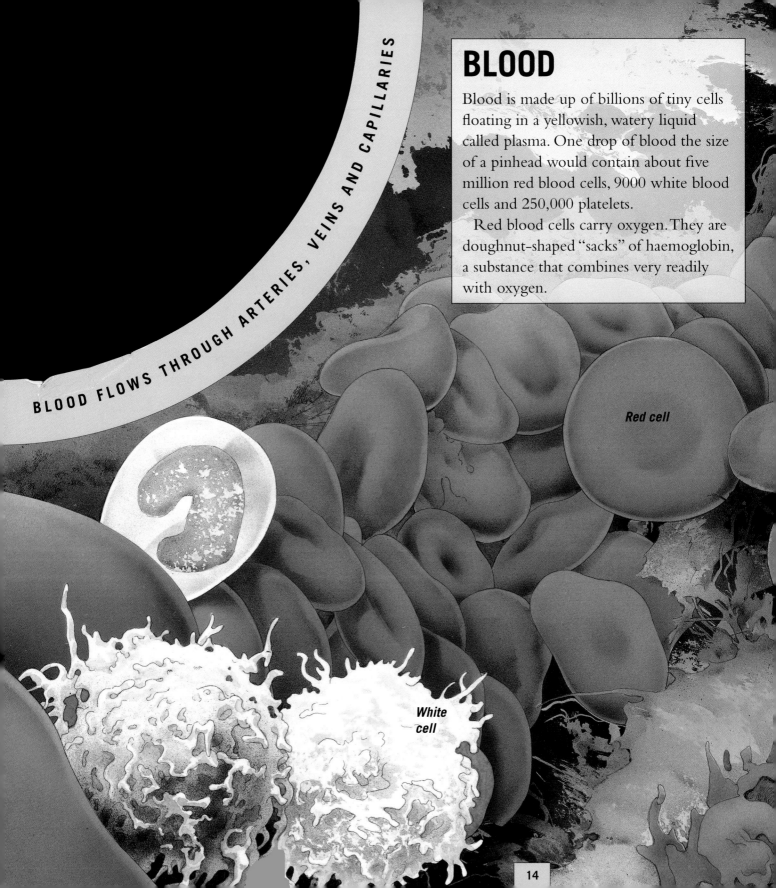

# BLOOD

Blood is made up of billions of tiny cells floating in a yellowish, watery liquid called plasma. One drop of blood the size of a pinhead would contain about five million red blood cells, 9000 white blood cells and 250,000 platelets.

Red blood cells carry oxygen. They are doughnut-shaped "sacks" of haemoglobin, a substance that combines very readily with oxygen.

*Red cell*

*White cell*

White cells are like a small army, ready to fight off infection from invading bacteria and viruses. Different types of white cells work together to do this: T-cells identify the invaders, B-cells make deadly substances called antibodies that surround the invaders, while macrophages engulf them and destroy them.

Platelets are fragments of cells. They help make the blood clot when a blood vessel is damaged (say by a mosquito bite), and so stop it from leaking out.

Platelet

White cell

TAKE A CLOSER LOOK AT THE INSIDE OF A WHITE BLOOD CELL

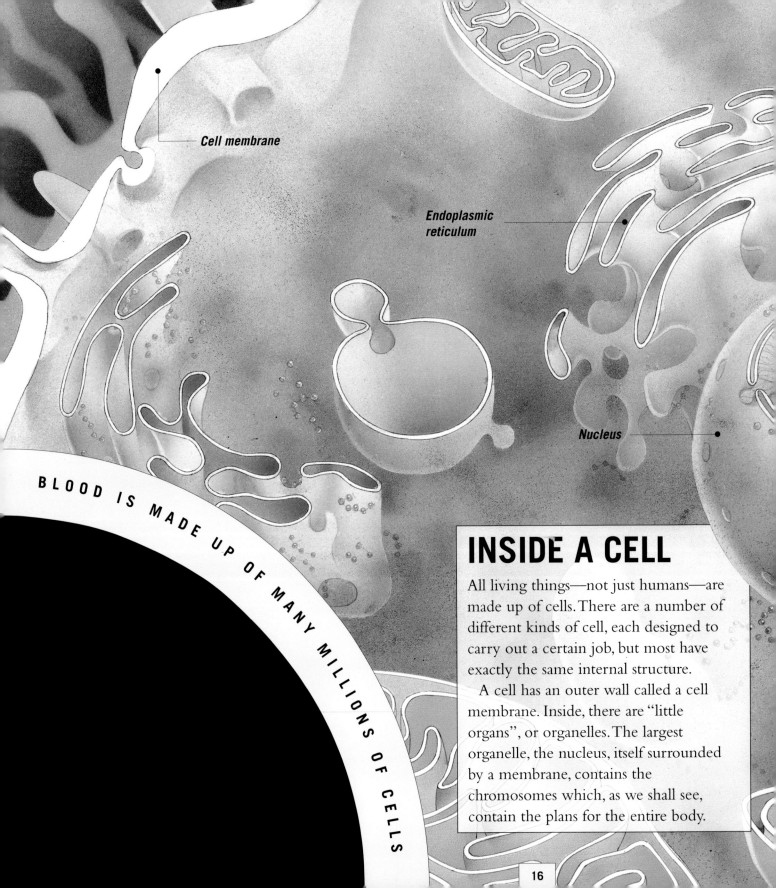

Cell membrane

Endoplasmic
reticulum

Nucleus

# INSIDE A CELL

All living things—not just humans—are
made up of cells. There are a number of
different kinds of cell, each designed to
carry out a certain job, but most have
exactly the same internal structure.

A cell has an outer wall called a cell
membrane. Inside, there are "little
organs", or organelles. The largest
organelle, the nucleus, itself surrounded
by a membrane, contains the
chromosomes which, as we shall see,
contain the plans for the entire body.

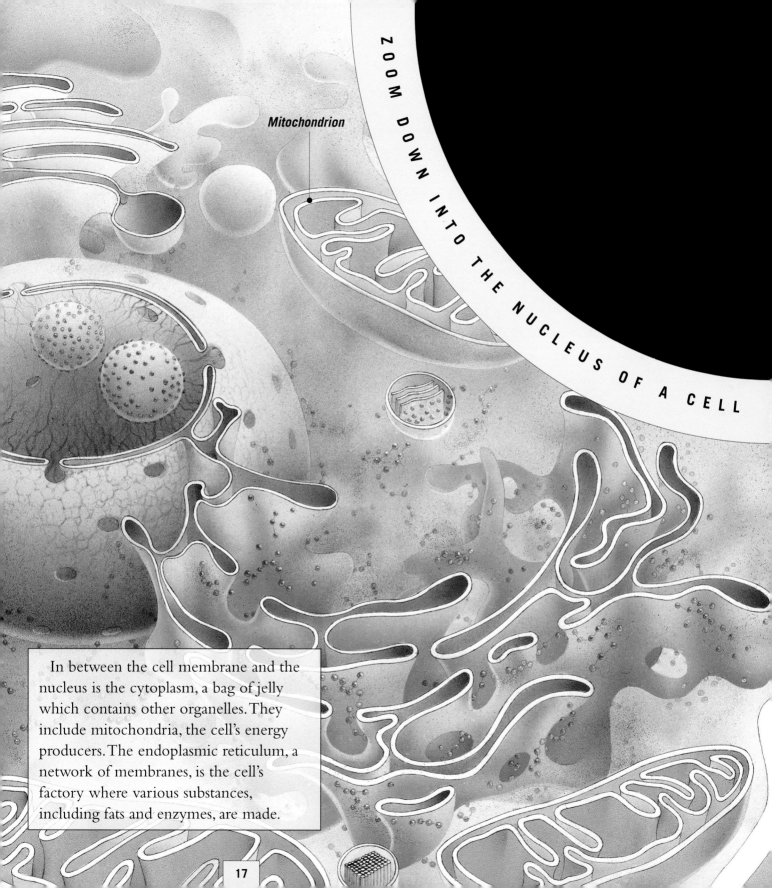

*Mitochondrion*

In between the cell membrane and the nucleus is the cytoplasm, a bag of jelly which contains other organelles. They include mitochondria, the cell's energy producers. The endoplasmic reticulum, a network of membranes, is the cell's factory where various substances, including fats and enzymes, are made.

# CHROMOSOMES

Genes contain all the information a living thing needs to develop, grow and maintain itself. The genes are found in the make-up of DNA (deoxyribonucleic acid), an extremely long, thin molecule that twists around protein cores. DNA and proteins are coiled tightly together to make thread-like fibres. When a cell divides *(see page 21)* each fibre is, itself, "super-coiled" into a short rod called a chromosome. Humans have 46 chromosomes in each cell nucleus.

Protein

DNA

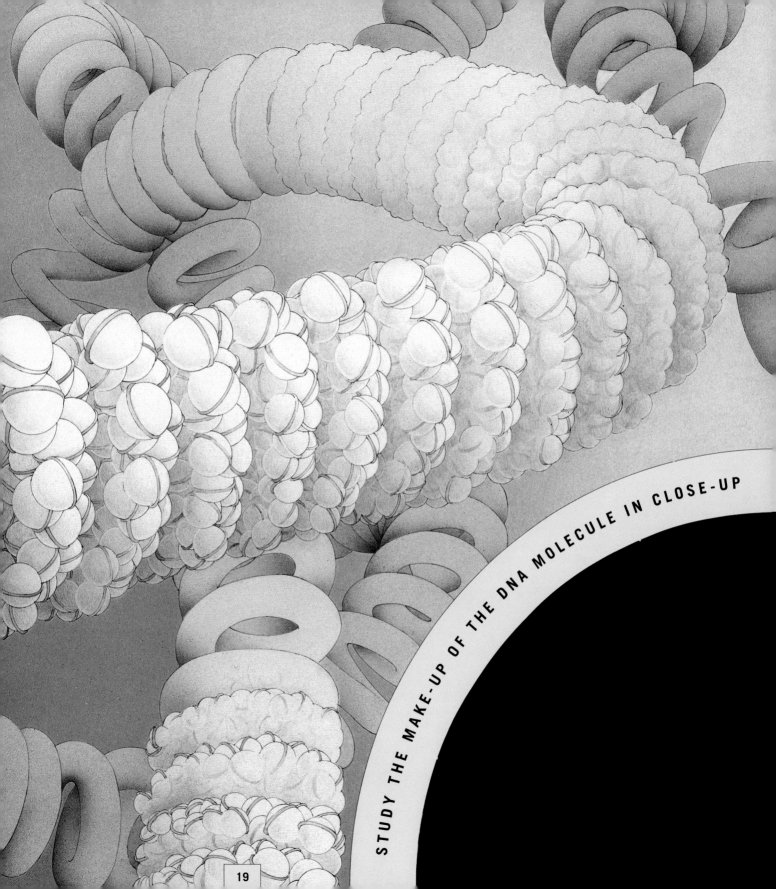

STUDY THE MAKE-UP OF THE DNA MOLECULE IN CLOSE-UP

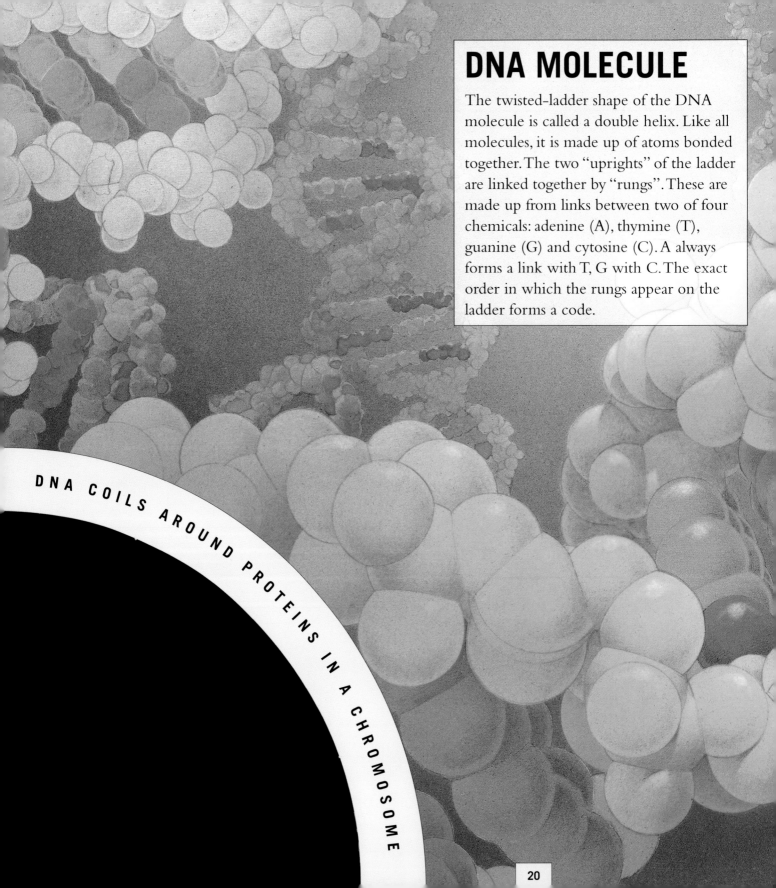

# DNA MOLECULE

The twisted-ladder shape of the DNA molecule is called a double helix. Like all molecules, it is made up of atoms bonded together. The two "uprights" of the ladder are linked together by "rungs". These are made up from links between two of four chemicals: adenine (A), thymine (T), guanine (G) and cytosine (C). A always forms a link with T, G with C. The exact order in which the rungs appear on the ladder forms a code.

DNA COILS AROUND PROTEINS IN A CHROMOSOME

A gene consists of a length of DNA with thousands of rungs. The code is detailed enough to provide instructions for making proteins, which provide the material for building cells. The human body has more than 30,000 genes.

Every minute, the body makes about three billion new cells as old ones die. When a cell divides to make two new cells, its DNA unzips itself along the line where the rungs are linked together. Each single strand then makes a new "partner" which is an exact copy of its old one.

*"Upright"*

*"Rung"*

*The DNA molecule consists of thousands of atoms (represented here by coloured balls) bonded together*

# THE DIGESTIVE SYSTEM

You need food to provide energy for your body. The things you eat must first be broken down into substances your body can use. This process is called **digestion**. It begins in the mouth, where the tongue and teeth make the food ready for swallowing. Saliva softens the food, making it easier to chew. The softened ball of food is pushed along the **oesophagus** down into the **stomach**.

Digestive juices in the stomach, including acids and special chemicals called **enzymes**, turn the food into a mush. Helped on its way by the squeezing action of muscles in the stomach, the food passes into the **intestines**. Here, more enzymes are poured into it (some from the **pancreas**). Vital nutrients are floated off and taken through the walls of the intestines into the bloodstream. Anything that cannot be digested is channelled into the **colon** (large intestine).

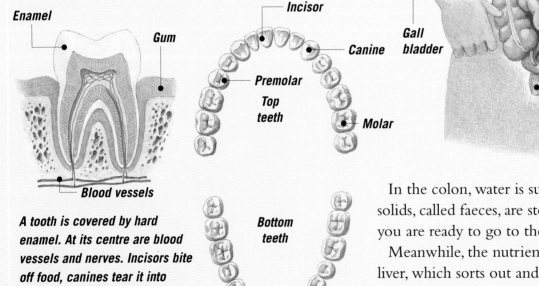

Saliva glands

Tongue

Teeth

Oesophagus

Liver

Stomach

Pancreas

Colon

Small intestine

Gall bladder

Rectum

Enamel

Gum

Blood vessels

Incisor

Canine

Premolar

Top teeth

Molar

Bottom teeth

*A tooth is covered by hard enamel. At its centre are blood vessels and nerves. Incisors bite off food, canines tear it into small pieces, while molars and premolars grind it up.*

In the colon, water is sucked away and the waste solids, called faeces, are stored in the **rectum** until you are ready to go to the toilet.

Meanwhile, the nutrients are ferried away to the liver, which sorts out and stores the substances needed by the body. Any waste is sent on in the bloodstream to the kidneys.

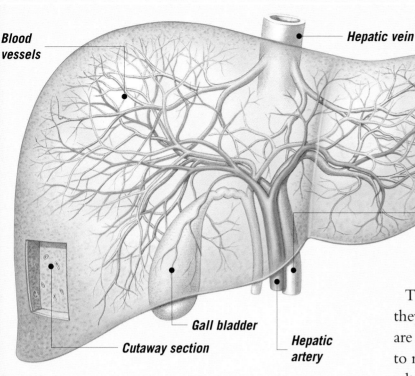

**Blood vessels**

**Hepatic vein**

**Portal vein**

**Gall bladder**

**Cutaway section**

**Hepatic artery**

*Blood containing nutrients enters the liver (left) through the portal vein, which connects to millions of tiny lobules. Here all the processing and waste disposal work is done. The treated blood is then taken to the hepatic vein, and from there on to the heart and to the rest of the body.*

Every drop of blood coming from the intestines must pass through the **liver** before it goes anywhere else. The liver acts as a kind of food processor and waste disposal unit combined. It makes new chemicals from the nutrients it receives in the blood from the small intestine, storing them until they are required. It also removes substances the body does not need.

For example, sometimes there are more nutrients from foods rich in protein (such as meat) than the body needs. The liver changes some of these into carbohydrates, to give energy, while the rest go into a waste substance called urea, which is sent to the kidneys, from where it leaves the body in urine.

The liver also collects up old, worn-out red blood cells and cleans out poisons, drugs, alcohol and other impurities from the bloodstream. Some of the chemical waste is turned into bile, which is stored in the **gall bladder.** This empties out back in the small intestine where it helps the digestive process.

The **kidneys** act as the blood's washing machine: they take out all the substances in the blood that are not needed, allowing only the useful substances to remain. They also control the levels of water and salts in the blood. The kidneys can filter about a quarter of the body's blood in about one minute.

Inside each kidney *(below)* there are a million tiny filters, called **nephrons**, through which blood passes. Waste, salt and water dribble down a tube called the **ureter** to the bladder, where they are stored ready to be passed out of the body as urine.

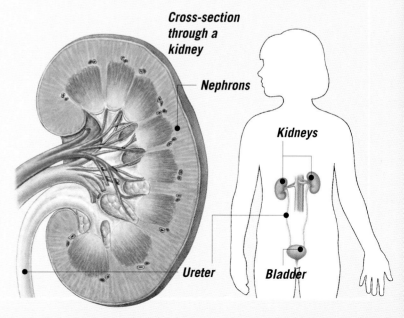

*Cross-section through a kidney*

**Nephrons**

**Kidneys**

**Ureter**

**Bladder**

# THE TRANSPORT SYSTEM

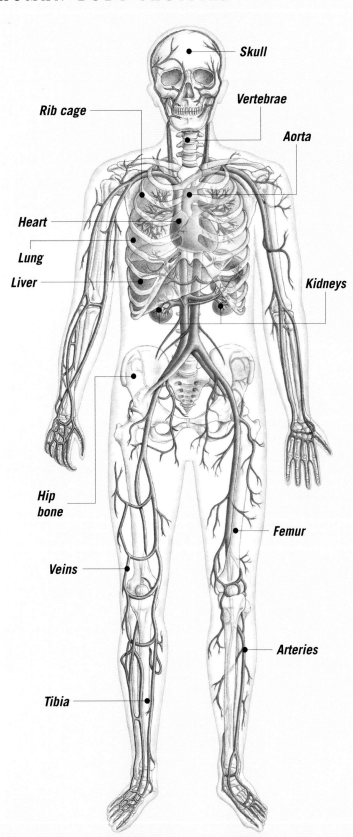

- Skull
- Vertebrae
- Rib cage
- Aorta
- Heart
- Lung
- Liver
- Kidneys
- Hip bone
- Femur
- Veins
- Arteries
- Tibia

All the muscles and tissues that make up the body must be continually supplied with food and oxygen. The job of transporting these essentials is done by the **blood vessels** *(left)*. Pumped by the heart, blood picks up dissolved food from the liver and oxygen collected from the lungs, then delivers them to all parts via the arteries. Veins carry blood together with carbon dioxide from the organs back to the heart. Blood also clears away waste, cools the body when it overheats, clots when the skin is damaged and protects against germs.

The heart pumps oxygen-rich blood from the lungs to the rest of the body, while pushing through oxygen-poor blood back to the lungs.

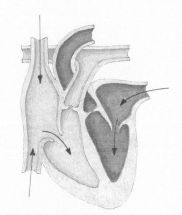

*The heart is like a powerful pump. As the heart muscles relax, blood is sucked in: oxygen-rich blood from the lungs (shown in red) and oxygen-poor blood from the rest of the body (blue).*

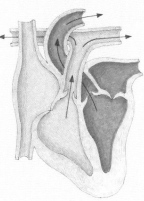

*Once inside the heart, flaps, called valves, prevent any blood from leaking back again. The heart then squeezes and pumps the blood out. The oxygen-rich blood goes to the rest of the body while the oxygen-poor blood goes to the lungs.*

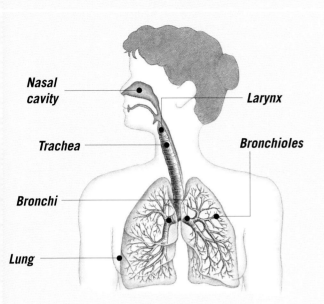

Nasal cavity

Larynx

Trachea

Bronchioles

Bronchi

Lung

*Two straps, the vocal cords, lie across the voice box, called the larynx. To speak, muscles pull them together so that there is only a very narrow slit between them. Air rushing through the slit makes them vibrate, producing sounds.*

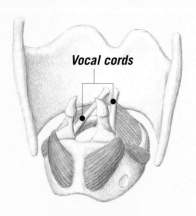

Vocal cords

# THE BREATHING SYSTEM

You need to breathe in oxygen from the air to live. From the nose or mouth, oxygen passes to the **lungs** via your **trachea** (wind-pipe). The trachea splits into two **bronchi**—one for each lung—which in turn divide into smaller **bronchioles**. These lead to millions of tiny air sacs called **alveoli**. The lungs are also linked to blood vessels from the heart. They divide into many capillaries, which form networks around the alveoli. The walls of both alveoli and capillaries are so thin that gases can seep through in both directions. Fresh oxygen from the air replenishes the blood arriving from the heart. Crossing the opposite way is the waste gas carbon dioxide (as well as water vapour). When you breathe out, this makes the return journey along the bronchioles to the trachea and out into the open air.

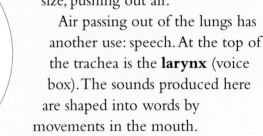

Bronchiole

Alveoli

Capillaries

You breathe by using your **diaphragm**, a sheet of muscle lying beneath the lungs, and the intercostal muscles between the ribs. To breathe in, the diaphragm is pulled down and the rib cage pulled out, making the lung cavity bigger. Air is sucked in to fill the space. To breathe out, the muscles are relaxed, the diaphragm moves up and the lungs return to their former size, pushing out air.

Air passing out of the lungs has another use: speech. At the top of the trachea is the **larynx** (voice box). The sounds produced here are shaped into words by movements in the mouth.

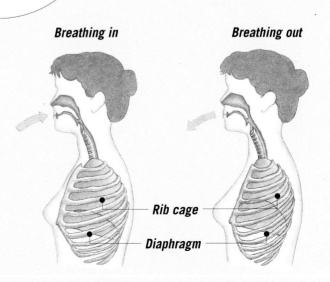

Breathing in

Breathing out

Rib cage

Diaphragm

# THE NERVOUS SYSTEM

Every thought and idea happens inside your **brain**. Protected inside your skull, it is linked, via the **spinal cord**, to a network of nerves leading to all the body's organs and muscles. It constantly receives information in the form of nerve signals, which it analyses and acts upon. It then issues instructions, deciding, for example, on your breathing rate, how you think and move, and many other tasks.

The brain has three main parts *(below)*. The **brain stem** at the base tapers into the spinal cord. It monitors the heartbeat, breathing, blood pressure, digestion and other vital activities. The second part is the cerebellum, a wrinkled lump at the rear of the brain. It deals with muscle control to make movements smooth and co-ordinated.

The third part is the forebrain. This is made up chiefly of the cerebrum, which accounts for 85 per

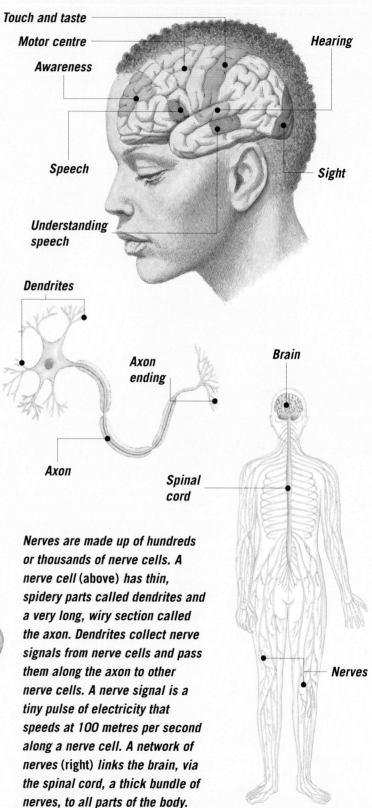

Nerves are made up of hundreds or thousands of nerve cells. A nerve cell *(above)* has thin, spidery parts called dendrites and a very long, wiry section called the axon. Dendrites collect nerve signals from nerve cells and pass them along the axon to other nerve cells. A nerve signal is a tiny pulse of electricity that speeds at 100 metres per second along a nerve cell. A network of nerves *(right)* links the brain, via the spinal cord, a thick bundle of nerves, to all parts of the body.

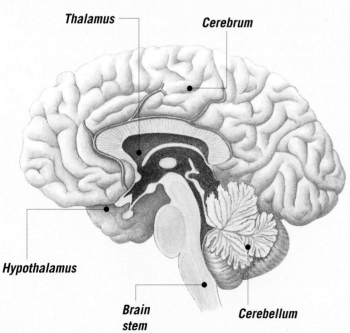

cent of the brain's bulk. The cerebrum's outer layer, called the **cerebral cortex**, is where most thoughts and ideas occur. The forebrain also includes the thalamus and hypothalamus. The **thalamus** acts as a relay station between the spinal cord and the cerebrum, sorting the nerve signals that run between them. The **hypothalamus** controls body temperature, hunger and other automatic functions.

The cerebral cortex, the outer layer of the cerebrum, has different areas, called centres, that deal with nerve signals coming from and going to different body parts *(opposite)*. For example, signals from the eyes are sorted and analysed in the sight centre at the lower rear of the brain. The centres that control the various muscles in the body are called the motor centres.

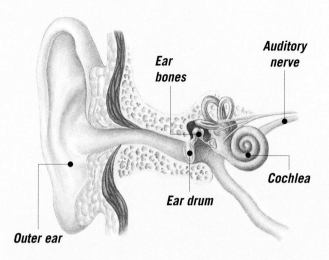

*Sound vibrations in the air strike the eardrum, a piece of skin in the ear* (above). *The vibrations are passed on to the tiny hammer, anvil and stirrup bones. Hairs inside the cochlea pick up the vibrations. They produce signals that travel along a nerve to the brain.*

*The tongue's upper surface* (below) *is covered with hundreds of pimple-like lumps, called papillae. Scattered between them are about 8000 taste buds. They can detect four basic tastes—sweet, sour, salty and bitter. Different parts of the tongue sense them.*

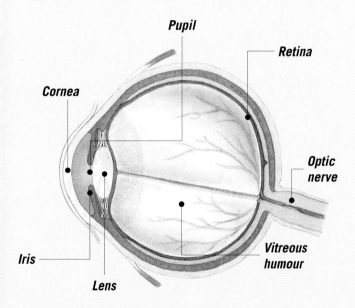

*Light enters the eye* (above) *through a transparent, domed window, called the cornea. It then passes through an opening, called the pupil, in the iris, the eye's coloured part. The iris is a ring of muscle that controls the size of the pupil, and so the amount of light that is allowed to enter the eye. Behind the iris there is a soft, elastic lens which focuses an image exactly on to the retina. From here, signals are sent along the optic nerve to the brain.*

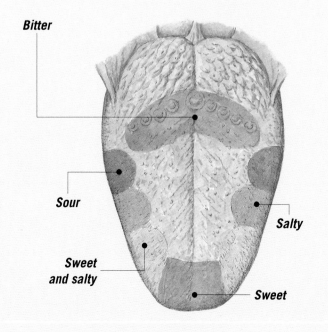

# THE SKELETON

Your skeleton supports your body and protects your vital organs. It is made up of 206 bones, each of which forms a rigid support and an anchorage point for muscles. Bones are made of a limestone-like substance that is four times stronger than concrete. Most bones are hollow with a cavity inside containing a soft, jelly-like substance called marrow, through which run blood vessels and nerves.

Bones are linked together at **joints**. In some, known as suture joints, the bones are fixed together and cannot move. In a movable joint, the ends of the bones are covered with a smooth, slippery substance called **cartilage**. Different joints allow certain kinds of movement. The knee, for example is a hinge joint, moving only backwards and forwards. Joints are held in place by flexible straps called **ligaments**.

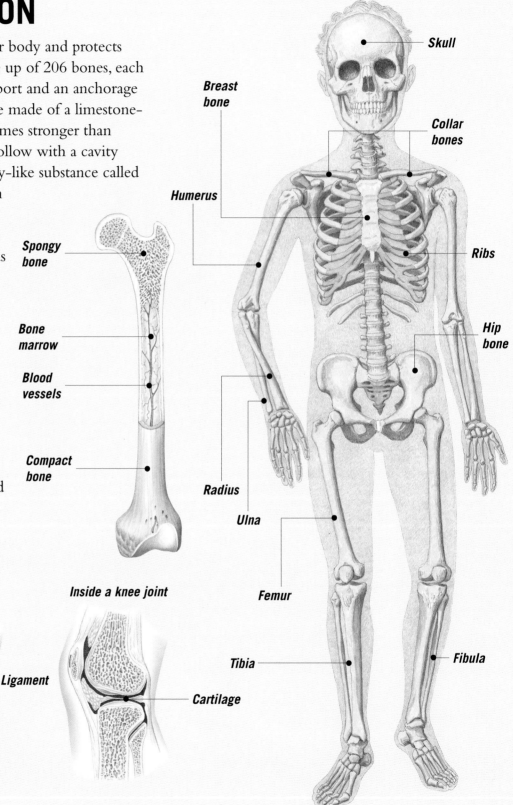

**Spongy bone**

**Bone marrow**

**Blood vessels**

**Compact bone**

**Skull**

**Breast bone**

**Collar bones**

**Humerus**

**Ribs**

**Hip bone**

**Radius**

**Ulna**

**Femur**

**Tibia**

**Fibula**

*Knee joint*

**Femur**

**Knee cap**

**Cartilage**

**Shin bone**

**Ligament**

*Inside a knee joint*

**Cartilage**

# THE MUSCLES

*Your muscles keep you upright and provide the force to allow you to move (right). The tendons, the tough cords that bind the muscle fibres to the bone supply the actual movement. Combinations of muscles, sometimes hundreds at a time, tilt and twist your bones in almost any direction.*

Every movement the body makes is powered by muscles. We can control most of our muscles. But some, such as those that move food in the intestines, we cannot control.

A muscle is a body part that is designed to get shorter. It can only pull on a bone, not push it. To move a limb, muscles must work in pairs. To bend your arm at the elbow *(below)*, the biceps shortens, pulling the lower arm. To straighten it, the triceps shortens and pulls as the biceps relaxes.

*Below is a cross-section through a typical piece of skin (see page 8). Skin has two layers. The outer layer, the epidermis, constantly renews itself as the dead surface material flakes away. The thicker, lower layer, the dermis, contains blood vessels, sweat glands, hair follicles (the pits surrounding the roots) and nerve endings. These can detect touch, heat, cold and pain. The messages sent to the brain or the spinal cord are designed to prevent damage to the body.*

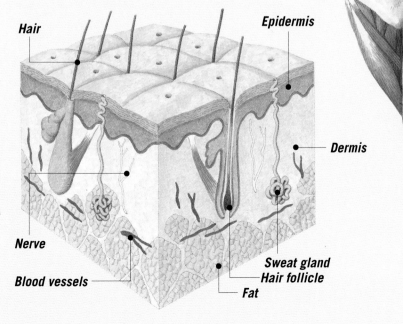

Hair
Epidermis
Dermis
Nerve
Blood vessels
Sweat gland
Hair follicle
Fat

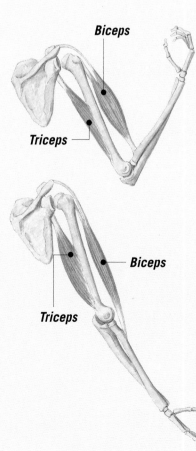

Biceps
Triceps
Biceps
Triceps

# GLOSSARY

**Alveoli** Tiny air sacs in the lungs where oxygen is taken up by the blood and carbon dioxide is released into the lungs and breathed out.

**Antibody** A substance carried in the blood which helps destroy unwanted bacteria and viruses.

**Artery** A tube which carries blood away from the heart. Most carry oxygen-filled blood to the body's organs and tissues but the pulmonary artery, which runs from the heart to the lungs, carries blood with very little oxygen in it.

**Bacteria** Tiny living things made up of only one cell. They can only be seen through a powerful microscope. Some bacteria live inside other cells. Some types cause disease.

**Capillaries** The smallest type of blood vessels, whose walls are only one cell thick.

**Cell** A tiny "building block" which makes up all the tissues in all living things. The blood provides it with nutrients and oxygen and removes waste from it. A cell is like a miniature factory, producing proteins and many other vital substances.

**Chromosome** A tiny, thread-shaped body inside the nucleus of a cell. Chromosomes are made of tightly-wound strands of DNA and proteins.

**DNA** (short for deoxyribonucleic acid) A molecule found in chromosomes, whose structure encodes a living thing's genes.

**Enzyme** A substance, usually a kind of protein, that speeds up chemical reactions. Enzymes help the body to digest food and obtain energy from it.

**Genes** The instructions contained in the chromosomes and which are passed from parent to offspring. Because they control the way in which all the cells are built, they determine a living thing's characteristics.

**Membrane** A thin, sheet-like tissue that lines body parts or organs.

**Molecule** A combination of atoms of different types bonded together. A molecule is the smallest part of a substance that can exist by itself and still possess its chemical properties.

**Nerve** A group of long, thin cells that carry messages between the brain and the rest of the body.

**Nutrients** Raw materials that a living thing must obtain in order to make and repair its body. For humans, nutrients are: proteins, carbohydrates, fats, vitamins and minerals.

**Organ** A structure made of different kinds of cells which does a particular job in the body. The brain, stomach and skin are all examples of organs.

**Proteins** Chemical substances found in all living things that carry out many essential tasks. For example, in humans, they form enzymes, which allow chemical processes to take place; they make up other substances that protect against diseases; they are found in muscles, skin and cartilage.

**Vein** A tube which carries blood to the heart. Most carry blood drained of oxygen but the pulmonary vein, which runs from the lungs to the heart, carries blood with fresh oxygen in it.

**Virus** A tiny, disease-carrying living thing, visible only under a powerful microscope. Viruses can only reproduce themselves inside the cell of another living thing.

# INDEX